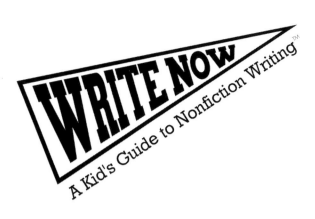

Writing to
RETELL

Jill Jarnow

The Rosen Publishing Group's
PowerKids Press™
New York

Published in 2006 by The Rosen Publishing Group, Inc.
29 East 21st Street, New York, NY 10010

First Edition

Editor: Frances E. Ruffin
Book Design: Emily Muschinske

Photo Credits: Cover and title page (girl) © Claudia Kunin/CORBIS, (boy, lower right) © Royalty-Free/CORBIS, (boy, upper left) © Rob Lewine/CORBIS; p. 5 © Royalty-Free/CORBIS; p. 7 © Doug Wechsler; p. 11 © North Wind Picture Archives; p. 15 © Royalty-Free/CORBIS; p. 19 © North Wind Picture Archives.

Library of Congress Cataloging-in-Publication Data

Jarnow, Jill.
Writing to retell / Jill Jarnow.— 1st ed.
    p. cm. — (Write now: a kid's guide to nonfiction writing)
Includes bibliographical references and index.
ISBN 1-4042-2836-5 (lib bdg.) — ISBN 1-4042-5317-3 (pbk.)
1. English language—Composition and exercises—Study and teaching (Early childhood) 2. Report writing—Study and teaching (Early childhood) 3. First person narrative—Study and teaching (Early childhood) I. Title.
LB1139.5.L35J36 2005
372.62'3—dc22

                                        2003018592

Manufactured in the United States of America

Contents

Writing to Retell

Have you ever put off writing a report for school because you didn't know where to start? In this book you will learn the skills that you need to turn your project from an idea into a written paper.

Many school writing projects are **nonfiction narratives**. This kind of writing requires retelling facts. A fact is information that can be proven. Writing a newspaper story often **involves** retelling the facts about a person, a place, or an event. Writing about events that occurred in the past is retelling history. A report that retells the life of another person is a biography. A story about yourself is an autobiography.

Clippings That Retell

Dog Owners Win Right to Use Park

Campers Rescue Lost Hikers

Losing Soccer Team Hires New Coach

File This...

Look in a magazine or a newspaper for examples of writing. Find biographies or nonfiction stories that you like. You can also look for articles in which someone is interviewed, or questioned. You might find them interesting. Make copies of these articles, or ask permission to clip them from the magazine or the paper. Place the clippings in a folder. As you write your own nonfiction articles, use your clippings to serve as examples of good writing.

Let's Get Resourceful

You have a great idea for a story that you would like to retell. Now you need to find **resources** that can provide good information about your subject. Your school and public libraries are among the best places to begin researching any subject.

All libraries have nonfiction books, encyclopedias, and almanacs. These are books or sets of books that are filled with facts. You will also find biographical dictionaries of famous people, and atlases, which are books filled with maps. You can do research on the Internet, too. Once you have your resources, take notes about the facts that you need to retell your story.

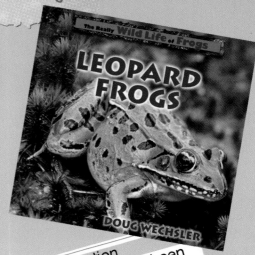

Each nonfiction book is given a call number that describes where it is located on the library shelves. When you find a book that you want to read in a catalog, write down the call number so that a librarian can help you find it.

Fairfield Public Library	Copies	Material	Location
J597.8 W	1	Book	Material has been checked/charged out

Personal Author **Wechsler, Doug.**

Title **Leopard frogs / Doug Wechsler.**

author

title

subject

Edition **1st ed.**

Publication info **New York : PowerKids Press, 2002.**

Physical descrip **24 p. : col. ill. ; 24 cm.**

Series **(The really wild life of frogs)**

Held by **FFLD-MAIN**

Subject term **Leopard frogs-- Juvenile literature.**

Subject term **Leopard frogs.**

Subject term **Frogs.**

This section tells you if the book has been checked out, or if it is available. Some books that cannot be borrowed are stored on special shelves. You might even be required to fill out cards to read them at a table in the library.

7

Writing a Report That Retells

There are five main steps to writing a report that retells. First research your subject and take notes. Next organize your notes and select the best facts to make an **outline**.

Write a **draft**, using your outline and notes. A first draft is about putting your ideas on paper. You will fix mistakes later. Next read, **revise**, and reread. It might help to read your draft aloud to hear how it sounds. Then correct any errors in **grammar** and spelling. Mark the changes on your draft and reread it. Keep revising until you like the way it sounds. Make a neat copy for your final draft. Neatness counts!

Writing Sample

The Jones Family Newsletter

By Kevin Jones

Hello everyone,

It is my turn to write this year's newsletter.

There are some exciting events to report in this

year's newsletter. I am glad ~~it is my turn to write it~~ because I can tell

you all about the family reunion we had this

summer. It was at Cedar Point Amusement Park,

the roller coaster capital of the world, in

Sandusky, Ohio! There was great turnout this
~~We had a fun~~

year, and it was great to see Grandpa Jim ride

Top Thrill Dragster, the world's tallest and

fastest roller coaster. It is 420 feet (128 m) tall

and reaches the speed of 120 miles (193 km) per

hour. Jim seems to have forgotten that he just

~~had his eightieth birthday this June!~~ Grandpa Jim

also had his eightieth birthday this June. For

those of you who could not make it this year, we

look forward to seeing you next time.

Look over your first draft and use the checklist to help you revise it.

Write a strong opening sentence.

Correct your spelling, punctuation, and grammar.

Cut facts that are repeated.

Write a satisfying closing sentence.

Checklist

- ✔ Write a strong opening sentence.
- ✔ Write a satisfying closing sentence.
- ✔ Rearrange events that are in the wrong place.
- ✔ Cut facts that are repeated.
- ✔ Correct your spelling, punctuation, and grammar.
- ✔ Recopy or retype your report to make it neat.

Use Timelines That Retell

A timeline can be a great way to organize and retell information. A timeline is a listing of events in the order in which they happened. Timelines work well as a way to retell information for biographical or historical **topics**. They can be used for any subject in which events take place over time. You could make a timeline of your life or the history of your school. No matter what your topic is, be sure your timeline includes all the important events for your subject.

A Timeline for Abigail Adams
by Sandra Harris

Make sure you title your work and write your name on it.

1744	Abigail Smith is born.
1764	Abigail Smith and John Adams are married.
1765	John and Abigail's first child, Abigail, is born.
1767	John Quincy Adams is born.
1768	Susanna Adams is born.
1770	Charles Adams is born. Susanna Adams dies in February.
1772	Thomas Boylston Adams is born.
1773	The Tea Act is passed and the Boston Tea Party happens.
1775	The American Revolution begins.
1783	The American Revolution ends. America wins independence from Britain.
1789	John is elected first vice president of the United States.
1797	John becomes the second president of the United States. Abigail becomes the first lady.
1818	Abigail Adams dies at home in Quincy, Massachusetts.

Timelines should list events in the order in which they happened. You can be as detailed in a timeline as you wish.

Be sure to include details about important events that might have had an effect on your subject.

Gathering Facts by Interviewing

Some of the best research for reports that retell may not be in books or online. Often an **expert** is a great source for hard-to-find information. To **interview**, or question, an expert, such as an artist, a scientist, or a historian, call the person or write a letter. Introduce yourself and explain the information that you need. Set a time and date to hold your interview. Prepare a list of questions. Make sure that you have a tape recorder, a few pencils, and a notebook ready for the interview. Take notes as you listen. If you hear an unfamiliar word, ask to have it explained. Go over your notes with the person before you end the interview.

An Interview with Louis Richards, a Social Worker

by Lisa Ruiz

Plan a list of questions before you meet with the person. Be sure to arrive for the interview or make your call on time.

What is your name?
Louis Richards.

Where do you work?
At the Philadelphia Department of Human Services.

Always begin an interview by asking for the person's name.

What is your job?
I am a social worker.

Why did you become a social worker?
I wanted a job where I could help kids.

What are some things that you do on your job?
I help children find foster homes. A foster home is often a home where children can live until they can join their own families.

Ask follow-up questions that provide details.

What else do you do?
I also help some children who don't have parents find people who will adopt them.

At the end of your interview, remember to thank the person for his or her time.

What kind of education do you need to do social work?
You must at least earn a degree from a four-year college.

Writing a Newspaper Article

A newspaper article is a story that retells. A newspaper article is written in an **inverted pyramid** and has five parts. The headline is the title of the article. It tries to catch a reader's interest. The first **paragraph** is the lead. It includes important information on the subject, such as the 5Ws.

The next paragraph is the bridge. It offers more **details** and moves readers from the lead to the body of the story. The body provides more supporting facts. The last paragraph should help readers to remember the article.

Write Right!

The 5Ws tell who, what, where, why, and when. Use these five pieces of information when you write to retell.

HIKERS LOST
ON BEAR CAVE MOUNTAIN

by David Smith

Michigan—Three hikers lost their way Saturday afternoon while climbing down the south side of Bear Cave Mountain. They had broken away from a larger group of hikers led by a tour guide.

Bear Cave Mountain has thick forests, deep valleys, and caves where animals are known to live. Over the years, several people have been lost while climbing its south side.

After a fifteen-hour search, the three lost hikers were discovered by a family of campers. The three had spent the night shivering inside a small cave. They were cold and wet from last night's thunderstorm, and were very hungry.

"I'm glad that I had half of a peanut butter sandwich and a few corn chips left from lunch," said Danny Wilson. "I shared it with the other guys, but it wasn't much. We were so hungry! We are glad to be found!"

Try not to end your article by writing "finally" or "at last." Use exciting language with quotations, or what people said, and active verbs.

Objective Reporting

Writing what is called a straight news story requires that your writing be objective. This means that as a **reporter** you must retell the facts and never write your own opinions. Opinions are your own beliefs about a subject or an event. The place for writing your opinions is in a personal **essay**. A reporter's job is to retell the facts of a story. If there are two possible sides to a story, he or she tries to present both sides. The reader can then form an opinion about what he or she has read, based on the complete picture. Keeping opinions and facts straight can be a tough job, but it is important in a nonfiction article.

Writing Exciting Headlines

Write a headline that will grab your reader's attention. A good headline uses strong action verbs, leaves out unnecessary words, and tells what the story is about.

Campers Find Lost Hikers

Losing Soccer Team Hires New Coach

Dog Owners Win Right to Use Park

Fact or Opinion?

Check out these examples of facts and opinions. Can you think of other examples of facts or opinions?

OPINIONS

Chocolate ice cream is the best.

Abigail Adams was the smartest and best first lady in American history.

The zoo is cool.

Everyone should visit Egypt.

FACTS

Ice cream must be kept in the freezer.

Abigail Adams was born in 1744.

The zoo is a place where one can visit many different animals.

People lived in Egypt more than 3,000 years ago.

17

Writing a Biography

A biography is a nonfiction story that you write about another person. Often you will be asked to write about the life of a famous or historic person. How can you make sure your "bio" is a story that people can't put down? If you need to, reread the text on page 8. Then choose a person you **admire**. Do thorough research about the person and his or her times. Write a timeline, then write a first draft. Describe important details, such as what people ate and wore, or what the schools were like. Details will bring this person and this time to life for your reader. Check your facts before using them in the biography.

A Biography

The Biography of Phillis Wheatley
by Michael Barnes

Phillis Wheatley was born in Africa in about 1761. European slave traders captured Phillis when she was about eight years old. They chained her on a boat with other African people. The boat sailed to Massachusetts, a colony in North America. Before it arrived, many people died at sea because the boat was hot and crowded and there was little food and water.

In Boston, Massachusetts, the Wheatley family bought Phillis as a slave. Most slaves were not taught to read or write. In those days many white people thought that black people could not be be educated in any way. Phillis proved them wrong. She learned to speak English, and the Wheatleys taught her to read and write. Soon Phillis began to write poetry. Mrs. Wheatley liked Phillis's poems. She arranged to have them printed in a magazine. Phillis became very famous. She was the first African American poet to have her poems printed.

Always add a title and sign your work.

Identify the person you are writing about. Include the person's birth date and the place in which he or she was born.

Give details that describe what the person went through.

Start a new paragraph when you begin writing about a new idea.

Writing a Memoir

Sometimes you may want to retell events that happened in your own life. This is called an autobiography. One kind of autobiography is called a memoir. Some memoirs may be accounts of one day from your memory, or about your memories of an older relative whom you admire. You may also write about a family vacation, or the time you made the winning goal during a soccer game.

The 5Ws will be important in writing a memoir, but try to include the five senses, too. Describe what you saw, heard, smelled, touched, and tasted. Can you think of three topics that would make good memoirs to write?

Writing a Memoir That Retells

Our Family Thanksgivings: A Memoir
by Jessica Starr

Thanksgiving Day is one of my favorite holidays. We always go to my grandparents' house on Webster Avenue. Before my family even gets out of the car, Grandmother is on the porch waving to us, saying, "Come on in. Everyone's here!"

As we hang up our coats, I can smell the turkey, sweet potato pies, grandmother's freshly baked rolls, and other good things to eat. My Grandfather, uncles, aunts, and cousins have gathered in the living room. Grandfather loves to tease my sisters and brothers and me. He calls us littlefolk. My brother Bobby plays the piano while the rest of us try to beat Grandfather at checkers.

At four o'clock, Grandmother tells us that dinner is ready and that we should sit at our places around the table. I sit at a smaller table for the younger kids, but I wish that I could sit at the grown-ups' table. Before we eat, we must each tell why we are thankful for this day. Then we eat until we are stuffed.

Introduce your topic. Remember the 5Ws as you write your memoir.

Try to use your five senses as you describe something in a memoir.

Add details that are personal to your memoir.

21

Keeping a Writer's Journal

A writer's journal can be one of the best tools that a person can have when writing to retell. It will allow you to remember the details of events that you experience. Your journal can be a notebook or a file on your computer. It does not matter how many words you write. After all, this is not an assignment. Look back at your entries every now and then. You will find that your writing skills have improved by retelling the events of your life in a journal.

Check It Out!

Using a writer's journal gives you a chance to try out different styles of writing. It can help to improve your writing skills.

Glossary

admire (ad-MYR) To respect or look up to.
details (DEE-taylz) Extra facts.
draft (DRAFT) A first written account of a story.
essay (EH-say) A short piece of writing written from a personal point of view.
expert (EK-spert) A person who knows a lot about a subject.
grammar (GRA-mer) The rules of how words combine to form sentences.
interview (IN-ter-vyoo) To question someone, usually an expert.
inverted pyramid (in-VERT-ed PEER-uh-mid) A piece of writing that contains most of the facts in the beginning.
involves (in-VOLVZ) Includes.
narratives (NAR-uh-tivz) Stories.
nonfiction (non-FIK-shun) Writing that is about people or events that are real.
outline (OWT-lyn) A written description that includes the main points of a paper.
paragraph (PAR-uh-graf) A group of sentences about a certain subject or idea.
reporter (ree-POR-ter) A person who writes or tells the news.
resources (REE-sors-ez) Supplies or useful things.
revise (rih-VYZ) To make changes to or improvements in something.
topics (TAH-piks) Subjects of pieces of writing.

Index

Web Sites

Due to the changing nature of Internet links, PowerKids Press has developed an online list of Web sites related to the subject of this book. This site is updated regularly. Please use this link to access the list:

www.powerkidslinks.com/wnkw/wretell/